NOV 2006

P9-DCU-702

Destination Detectives

Mexico

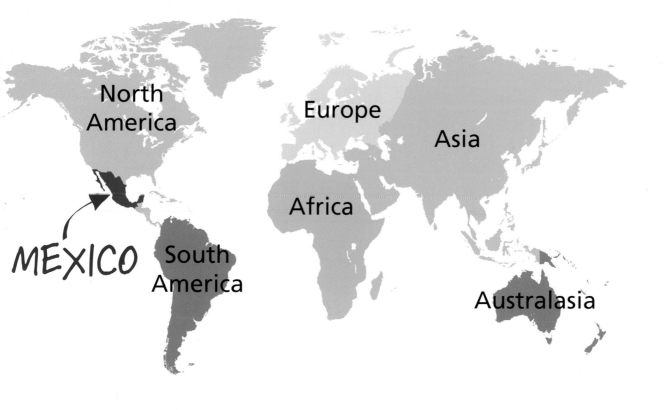

North
America

Europe

Asia

MEXICO

South
America

Africa

Australasia

Jen Green

Chicago, Illinois

3 1267 13940 3651

© 2006 Raintree
Published by Raintree,
A division of Reed Elsevier, Inc.
Chicago, Illinois

Customer Service 888–363–4266

Visit our website at www.heinemannraintree.com

All rights reserved. No part of this publication may be
reproduced or transmitted in any form or by any means,
electronic or mechanical, including photocopying, recording,
taping, or any information storage and retrieval system,
without permission in writing from the publisher.

Printed and bound in China WKT Company Limited

10 09 08 07 06
10 9 8 7 6 5 4 3 2 1

Library of Congress Cataloging-in-
Publication Data
Green, Jen.
  Mexico / Jen Green.
     p. cm. -- (Destination detectives)
  Includes bibliographical references.
  ISBN 1-4109-1866-1 (lib. bdg.)
  1. Mexico--Description and travel--Juvenile literature. 2.
Mexico--Geography--Juvenile literature. I. Title. II. Series.
  F1216.5.G73 2005
  917.2--dc22
                            2005011557

Acknowledgments
The author and publishers are grateful to the following
for permission to reproduce copyright material:
ABPL p. 18 (Tony Robins); Action Plus pp. 26-27 (Neil
Tingle); Alamy Images pp. 20r (Brian Atkinson), 43
(britishcolumbiaphotos.com), 20l (D. Hurst), 34 (Danita
Delimont), 30-31 (John Arnold Images), 38-39 (PCL), 12-13
(Stock Connection); Bridgeman Art Library pp. 10 (Father
Hidalgo (mural), Orozco, Jose Clemente (1883-1949) /
Government Palace, Guadalajara, Mexico, Mexicolore), 10-11
(Museo Nacional de Historia, Mexico City, Mexico); Corbis
pp. 8 (Bettmann), 38 (Bob Krist), 24 (Bohemian Nomad
Picturemakers), 32-33 (Carl & Ann Purcell), pp. 9l, 22-23, 41
(Charles & Josette Lenars), pp. 16-17, 18-19, 21, 33, 40, 42
(Danny Lehman), 29 (Gerald French), 35 (Gideon Mendel),
5 (Gunter Marx Photography), 9r (Historical Picture Archive),
13 (Kevin Schafer), 12, 27, 36 (Macduff Everton), 16 (Nik
Wheeler), 15 (Owen Franken), 26 (Pablo San Juan), 28 (Phil
Schermeister), 31 (Randy Faris), 14-15 (Reuters), 36-37
(Robert Holmes), 42-43 (Stephen Frink), 24-25 (Steve Starr),
7t (Tom Bean); Corbis Royalty Free pp. 7b, 28-29;
Harcourt Education Ltd pp. 4-5, 6 (John Miller);
www.visitmexicopress.com pp. 23, 30.

Cover photograph of cactus reproduced with permission of
Corbis/B.S.P.I..

Illustrations by Kamae Design.

Every effort has been made to contact copyright holders
of any material reproduced in this book. Any omissions will
be rectified in subsequent printings if notice is given to the
publishers.

The paper used to print this book comes from
sustainable resources.

Disclaimer
All the Internet addresses (URLs) given in this book were valid
at the time of going to press. However, due to the dynamic
nature of the Internet, some addresses may have changed, or
sites may have changed or ceased to exist since publication.
While the author and publishers regret any inconvenience this
may cause readers, no responsibility for any such changes can
be accepted by either the author or the publishers.

Contents

Some words are shown in bold, **like this.** You can find out what they mean by looking in the glossary. You can also look out for them in the Word Bank box at the bottom of each page.

Mariachi music

Mariachi music has been popular in Mexico for more than a hundred years. The musicians play to crowds in town squares and cafés all over Mexico. Mariachi musicians play guitars, trumpets, and violins. They often wear a traditional costume including a sombrero and a poncho (see photo on p. 5).

You wake up in a hotel room to the sound of music and singing. Looking out, you see a narrow street with brightly colored buildings. A small band of musicians is strolling up the street!

Where are you?

It is still early, with the morning sun striking the domes of a church in the distance. A man dressed in a poncho (huge shawl-type garment) is selling fruit on the street below. Farther down, you can see a few shops with signs in Spanish.

A typical street in central Puebla, where your journey begins!

Strolling players

The musicians are now passing. There are two men strumming guitars and one playing a violin. They are singing a sad song with Spanish words. Their clothes give you a clue—they are all wearing broad-brimmed sombrero hats, short jackets, narrow pants, and cowboy boots.

This can only be Mexico! The musicians are one of the country's famous mariachi bands. When the song ends, you ask them some questions. You find out that you are in the city of Puebla in the Central Highlands of Mexico. You have arrived just in time for a big fiesta (festival), for which the musicians are warming up.

Ponchos and Sombreros

Ponchos are traditional clothes worn by Mexican farm workers. A poncho is a square of woven cloth with a hole to put your head through. Sombreros are wide-brimmed hats that shield the head from the sun.

▲ Ponchos keep out rain and provide warmth in chilly weather.

This is your first time in Mexico, and you don't know much about the country. The hotel has a tourist brochure, which includes a map of Mexico's different regions. You look at both over breakfast, when you have a *pan dulce*, a sweet roll.

Size and shape

With a land area of nearly 780,000 million square miles (nearly 2 million square kilometers), Mexico is the world's fourteenth-largest country. It is shaped like a funnel—widest in the north, where it borders the United States. Guatemala and Belize lie on the southern boundary.

Mexico includes two large **peninsulas**. In the west, Baja California stretches far into the Pacific Ocean. In the east, the diamond-shaped Yucatan Peninsula juts into the Gulf of Mexico.

Where do people live?

Mexico can be divided into three main regions:
- Much of the north is dry and **barren**, with few people.
- Most people live in the central area of the highlands. The capital, Mexico City, lies here, along with many other towns, including Puebla.
- The far south and the Yucatan Peninsula have fewer towns and villages.

Mexico Fact File

POPULATION:
104.9 million

AREA:
756,066 square miles (1,958,202 square kilometers)

CAPITAL:
Mexico City

LANGUAGES:
Spanish is the official language. There are more than 50 Mexican Indian languages.

CURRENCY:
The *peso is* made up of 100 *centavos.*

TYPE OF GOVERNMENT:
Federal republic. This is a country where all the different regions are self-governing, but united by a central government. There is not a monarch.

WORD BANK   **barren** bare land, with very little growing on it
colony country that is controlled by another ruling country

Mexico is divided into 31 states and a federal district. Each state has its own government and its citizens elect their governor. The Federal District is a special political region where the capital, Mexico City is located.

Huge varieties of cacti are a common sight in the dry north of Mexico.

UNITED STATES OF AMERICA

ake Salada

Baja California

Sonora

Chihuahua

Chihuahua

Coahuila

Baja California Sur

inaloa

Durango

Monterrey
Nuevo
Leon

Rio Grande

GULF OF CALIFORNIA

PACIFIC OCEAN

Zacatecas

San Luis Potosí

Tamaulipas

GULF OF MEXICO

Nayarit

Aguascalientes

Tequila

León

Queretaro

Hidalgo

Cancún

Yucatán

Tlaxacala

Quintana Roo

Campeche

CARIBBEAN SEA

Guadalajara

Jalisco

Colima

Mexico City

Puebla

Puebla

Veracruz

Tabasco

BELIZE

Guanajuato

Guerrero

Chiapas

HONDURAS

Michoacán

Acapulco

Oaxaca

Sierra Madre

Edo de Mexico

Morelos

Pico de Orizaba

GUATEMALA

N
W   E
S

0 ──────── 800 km
0 ──────── 500 miles

EL SALVADOR

Cancun, on the Yucatan Peninsula, is Mexico's most famous beach resort.

Mexico's Population

Mexico's original **inhabitants** were Mexican Indians, who spread south from North America more than 20,000 years ago. People arrived from Europe in the 1500s. For 300 years, Mexico was a Spanish **colony**. Now, most people are *mestizos*—people of mixed ancestry (see pie chart below).

Other (15%)

Mexican Indian (10%)

Mestizos (75%)

inhabitant   someone who lives in a place
peninsula   area of land that is mostly surrounded by water

7

History

Human Sacrifice

People in ancient Mexico were very religious. The Aztecs worshiped their Sun god by performing human **sacrifice**. They cut out the hearts of their victims and offered them to the god.

▲ The Aztecs believed that human sacrifice was necessary so that the Sun would rise every day.

After breakfast you take a look around Puebla. You see a strange hill with a church on top. Someone tells you it is the Great Pyramid of Cholula—the remains of an ancient temple.

You are here!

The tourist brochure tells you that Mexico was home to many great civilizations before 1600. They ruled mighty **empires** and built amazing cities that still stand in many parts of Mexico. First, were the Olmecs, who carved giant stone heads. Later, the Mayas built temples in the Yucatan. Last, were the Aztecs, who ruled much of Mexico from the 1300s to the 1520s. They were conquered by Spanish soldiers called conquistadors.

New Spain

The Spanish took over the Aztec empire and made it a Spanish **colony**. They captured more land to build a massive **territory** called New Spain. It included much of Central America, up to northern Panama, and much of the United States. All over Mexico the Spanish built European-style cities, with a square called the *zocalo* in the center. You wander in to the center of town to find Puebla's *zocalo*. You discover that the city was founded as Puebla in 1532.

empire group of countries ruled by a single country or ruler

The Spanish Conquest

In 1519 a Spanish soldier named Hernan Cortes arrived in Mexico in search of gold and silver. He brought a few hundred men, armed with guns and cannons. In less than three years the Spaniards had conquered the Aztecs.

This painting shows Hernan Cortes meeting the Aztec ruler, Montezuma. Montezuma was killed in 1520.

The Great Pyramid at Cholula was once the largest temple in Central America. Later, trees sprouted on it, and a church was built on top.

sacrifice something that is killed and offered to a god
territory land that a country or ruler owns or controls

In Puebla's main square you admire the Spanish cathedral. Continuing your stroll, you end up in the local Museum of the Revolution, which explains all about Mexico's more recent history.

Spanish rule

Mexico remained a Spanish **colony** for 300 years. During this time life was hard for the Mexican people. They had to work on the land or in the mines that supplied Spain with silver and gold. In 1810 a priest named Miguel Hidalgo y Costilla called upon Mexicans to overthrow the Spanish. His speech started a rebellion. In 1821, after eleven years of fighting, Mexico won its **independence** from Spain.

Viva Mexico!

In 1810 Father Miguel Hidalgo made a passionate speech from his church in Dolores in central Mexico, *Mexicanos, viva Mexico!* ("Mexicans, long live Mexico!") Every year Mexico's president repeats this rousing cry on Independence Day, which begins at 11 P.M. on September 15, which celebrates freedom from Spanish rule.

Hidalgo's speech is known as the *grito de Dolores*—cry from Dolores.

WORD BANK   cavalry soldiers on horses
dictator ruler who governs without having been elected by the people

Early years of independence

The first century of independence did not bring peace for Mexican people. Mexico fought wars with the United Kingdom, France, Spain, and the United States and lost more than half of its **territory** to the United States. A **dictator** named Porfirio Diaz ruled Mexico for around 30 years from 1876. In 1910, Mexicans rose up against him. This was the Mexican Revolution. The fighting lasted until 1917, when the revolutionaries won.

Land and Liberty!

Two soldiers led the Mexican Revolution. Francisco "Pancho" Villa was a bandit chief and a brilliant **cavalry** officer. Emiliano Zapata encouraged Mexicans using the slogan *Tierra y Libertad!* (Land and Liberty!)

In 1862 France invaded Mexico. Mexicans defeated the French at the Battle of Puebla. However, the French were victorious later the same year.

Underground Mexico

Mexico has lots of amazing cave systems, including many in the Yucatan Peninsula. Limestone-rich water dripping from cave roofs creates rocky stalactites hanging downward. Tall columns called stalagmites rise up from the floor.

From high up you can see that Puebla is ringed by mountains. Is the rest of Mexico similar? You study a **relief map** on display in a local shop.

Mountains and plateaus

Much of Mexico is mountainous, with over half the country above 3,300 feet (1,000 meters). There are two long chains of mountains, the western and eastern Sierra Madre. The Central **Plateau** in between covers a huge area, with cities such as Puebla found in **fertile** valleys. Even more mountain ranges lie in the far south and in Chiapas in the east.

Fact Box

Highest mountain: Pico de Orizaba, 18,696 feet (5,699 meters) above sea level
Lowest point: Lake Salada, 33 feet (10 meters) below sea level
Coastline: 5,830 miles (9,350 kilometers)

WORD BANK   fertile land that is good for growing crops on
plateau area of high, flat land

Rivers and lowlands

Mexico's longest river is the Rio Bravo (also called the Rio Grande). Flowing for 1,880 miles (3,025 kilometers), this river forms much of the border with the United States.

The Gulf Coast and Yucatan **Peninsula** are Mexico's biggest lowlands. In the Yucatan, water seeping through the **porous** limestone rock produces underground rivers. In some places, the roofs of these rivers have collapsed, creating rocky pools called *cenotes*.

Cenotes such as this one have clear blue waters. *Cenotes* were holy places in ancient times.

Copper Canyon

The *Barranca del Cobre* (Copper Canyon) is one of Mexico's most dramatic features. Located in the western Sierra Madre, it is made up of five linked canyons. Together they are five times wider, and one and a half times deeper, than the Grand Canyon in the United States.

Copper Canyon is a striking scene at sunset.

porous rock that has tiny holes so that water can trickle through it
relief map map that shows where the land is higher or lower

Birth of a Volcano

Mexico's youngest volcano, *Paricutin*, is less than a century old. It began life as a smoking mound in a farmer's field in 1943. Since then it has grown to a towering mountain more than 9,200 feet (2,800 meters) high.

The name *Popocatépetl* means "Old Smoky" in a local Indian language.

➤

Volcanoes and earthquakes

Whoa! What was that? For a second the ground seemed to shake, but no one took much notice. Someone says it was a tremor—a small earthquake. These are quite common in Mexico.

Out in the Pacific Ocean west of Mexico lies a deep **trench**. This trench is a boundary between two of the giant sections (called **tectonic plates**) that form Earth's outer layer. These plates meet and push together here. The enormous pressure causes earthquakes and volcanic eruptions in Mexico. Small tremors like the one you just felt are quite common. Major earthquakes hit from time to time.

WORD BANK   active volcano that may erupt sometime in the future
dormant volcano that is not expected to erupt again

Smoking volcano

A line of volcanic mountains runs west to east across Mexico not far from Puebla. They include two tall, cone-shaped peaks that tower over the city. *Iztaccíhuatl* (known as Izta) is a **dormant** volcano. Neighboring *Popocatépetl* (known as Popo) is **active**. You often see a plume of smoke rising from the mountain. In 1994 Popo showered Puebla with ash and in 2000 villagers were evacuated because of an eruption.

Hundreds of buildings collapsed in the 1985 earthquake.

Unlucky Capital

In 1985, a major earthquake hit Mexico City, destroying the city hospital, government buildings, and thousands of homes. More than 6,000 people died and many more were injured.

Too Much and Too Little

Only about 4 inches (10 centimeters) of rain a year falls in northern Mexico. Deserts stretch for hundreds of miles near the U.S. border. Parts of southern Mexico have the opposite problem. Heavy summer downpours in Chiapas and Tabasco can cause floods.

Weather in Mexico

The midday sun is fierce in Puebla. Everyone wears hats and sunglasses. Many people take a Spanish-style *siesta* (snooze) after lunch. Things cool down late in the afternoon.

Different climates

Height above sea level is the main thing that affects the **climate** in different parts of Mexico. The lowlands are the hottest areas, while high mountains are the coolest. Between the two, the Central **Plateau** has a mild climate, with warm summers and cool winters.

In parts of southeastern Mexico, up to 157 inches (400 centimeters) of rain falls yearly. The high rainfall allows lush forests to grow.

WORD BANK climate regular pattern of weather in a region
hurricane fierce storm with very high winds

Rainfall

Puebla gets quite a lot of rain, especially in summer. But many parts of Mexico get very little rain. As a result deserts and **scrubland** cover more than half of the country, mainly in the north.

Spreading deserts

The deserts of northern Mexico are getting larger. Experts think this is linked to the world's climate getting warmer. Farms in the north also use a lot of water, which is reducing the amount of water found underground.

Hurricane Season

The Gulf and Pacific coasts of southern Mexico are sometimes hit by **hurricanes** in late summer. These tropical storms form out at sea and then move inland causing great destruction. In 1995, coasts of the Yucatan were hit by two powerful hurricanes in the same year.

Mexico's highest mountain, Pico de Orizaba, shows the effect of height on climate. The top of the mountain is always covered in snow, while pine forests grow on lower slopes.

scrubland area covered in small trees and bushes

Food & Culture

It's now evening, and you're very hungry. Time to get to grips with Mexican cooking! Like much of Mexican culture, the local cooking is a mixture of Spanish and Indian. Tasty and often spicy, Mexican food is enjoyed around the world.

Tortillas and beans

Mexico's main food is corn, which is ground into cornmeal and made into flat pancakes called tortillas. These are served in many different ways, filled or topped with cheese, meat, and spices. Beans and chili are used in many dishes. Perhaps the most famous is chili con carne (meat and beans in a spicy sauce).

On the Menu

- Tacos: tortillas folded around fillings such as cheese, beans, vegetables, or meat with a spicy sauce
- Tostadas: flat tortillas toasted and piled with toppings such as cheese, beans, or spicy meat
- Guacamole: avocado dip
- Chiles rellenos: green chili peppers stuffed with cheese or meat and spices, and then fried and served with a sauce

Lettuce, avocado, and sour cream garnish this taco.

18

Eating out

Mexicans love to eat out in restaurants. In cities the main meal is served in the evening. In the country, it's more often eaten at lunchtime. Food may be washed down with fruit juice and adults may choose beer.

Foods of Mexico

Europeans brought chickens, pigs, goats, wheat, garlic, and apples to Mexico. In return, Mexican foods such as chocolate, vanilla, and chili peppers are now used in cooking worldwide. Tomatoes, avocados, beans, and peanuts also come from this part of the world.

Mole Sauce

Mole is a rich, dark sauce made of unsweetened chocolate, chili, and more than 30 herbs and spices. It is served with chicken and turkey. This sauce is said to have been invented right here in Puebla!

You can buy a huge variety of tasty snacks at almost any time of day in Mexico.

China Poblana

Legend says China Poblana arrived in Puebla as a slave, having been captured by pirates. The outfit she was wearing—a frilly blouse and embroidered skirt—became the traditional dress of Mexican women. It's now mainly worn on fiesta days.

Fiesta day

The next day is May 5, or *Cinco de Mayo*. This is the anniversary of the day in 1862 when Mexican soldiers beat the French at the Battle of Puebla. Celebrations go on all over Mexico, but the biggest are right here in Puebla.

Celebrations begin

The party begins early on fiesta day. A market springs up in the main square, selling handicrafts and special little snacks called *antojitos*. Wandering about town, you come across a church with a tomb inside. The tomb is supposed to be the grave of a 17th-century Asian princess called China Poblana. The national costume that many Mexican women still wear today was inspired by the way China Poblana dressed.

► Fireworks explode and firecrackers pop during the 5 May festival.

◄ Women show off their national costume during a parade at a fiesta.

In full swing

A rodeo is held on the edge of town in honor of the fiesta. Meanwhile celebrations heat up in the main square. There's a parade with everyone in costume, including feathery Indian headdresses. People dance to the music of mariachi bands.

Best of all are the fireworks. In some Mexican cities these are wired on to tall frames shaped like castles. Here in Puebla they're attached to a bull costume worn by a man who charges the crowd. Firecrackers explode everywhere—exciting but scary!

Rodeos

Charreadas (rodeos) are held on fiesta days. Cowboys (*charros*), in splendid outfits, ride wild bulls or bucking bronco horses. Others show their skill with the lasso by roping bulls and other horses as they ride (see left).

Religion and holidays

You go into a café to escape the fireworks! Several local people are there. You ask them about religion and festivals in Mexico.

Catholic saints

Mexico has no official religion, but most people (90 percent) are Roman Catholics. **Catholicism** arrived with the Spanish conquistadors in the 16th century. Mexico's best-loved saint is the Virgin of Guadalupe—the Virgin Mary, who is Mexico's **patron saint**. A big *posada* (procession) is held in her honor in Mexico City on her fiesta day, December 12.

Important Holidays and Fiestas

JANUARY 1:
New Year's Day

MARCH 21:
Birthday of Benito Juarez, one of Mexico's early presidents

MARCH/APRIL:
Lent and Easter

MAY 5:
Battle of Puebla

SEPTEMBER 15–16:
Independence Day

OCTOBER 12:
Columbus Day

NOVEMBER 1–2 :
Day of the Dead

NOVEMBER 20:
Revolution Day

DECEMBER 12:
Feast of Our Lady of Guadalupe

DECEMBER 25:
Christmas Day

These gruesome skulls are really quite sweet – they are made from chocolate and icing!

Catholicism the Roman Catholic religion, a form of Christianity

Mexican festivals

Some fiestas celebrate great dates in Mexico's history, such as May 5 and Independence Day, which starts at 11 P.M. on 15 September and continues long into the next day. Most fiestas are Catholic saints' days. However many Christian festivals also reflect traditional Indian beliefs.

Mexico's most famous fiesta, the Day of the Dead, is an example of this. On this day, Mexicans remember their dead relatives. Families prepare a feast and invite the spirits of the dead to attend. People light candles to guide the spirits home, and give sweets and chocolate in the shape of skulls.

Bulls on the Loose!

The town of Huamantla in southeastern Mexico has a scary bull-running festival called *La Noche en que Nadie Duerme* – "the night when no one sleeps." On this night, bulls run loose through streets covered with flowers and colored sawdust. When the bull heads toward you, you'll have to scramble to get out of the way!

The morning after the fiesta, it's back to normal life. Streets are crowded with adults and children heading to work or school. You talk to some of them about jobs and schools in Mexico.

Mining

Mexico is rich in **minerals** such as gold, silver, zinc, lead, and copper. There are large reserves of oil and natural gas both on land and offshore. Mining gives the country much of its wealth.

Jobs and industry

In Puebla the biggest employer is a car factory. Mexico has many factories. They produce everything from vehicles to iron and steel, chemicals, clothing, and processed foods. Mexico City and large towns such as Monterrey are major industrial centers. So are the factories called *maquiladoras*, located near the U.S. border. Here, American and Japanese companies employ Mexicans to make electronic equipment, clothes, and other products.

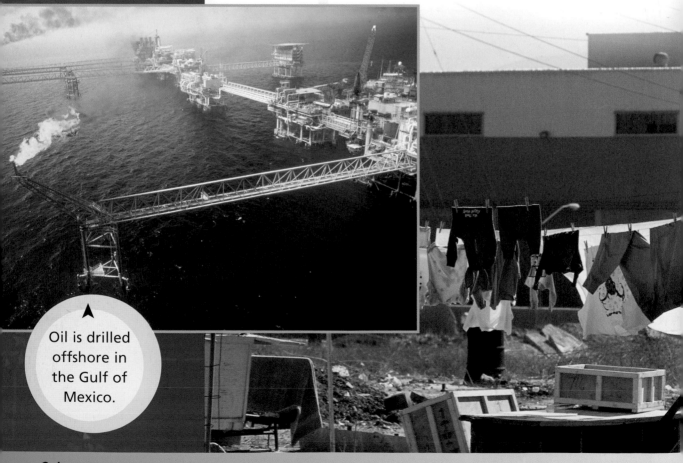

Oil is drilled offshore in the Gulf of Mexico.

Schools

Education is free and **compulsory** for everyone between the ages of five and eleven. The Mexican government encourages children to stay at school for at least another three years after this. But after age eleven, education is no longer free, and many poorer families cannot afford it.

Many children in the country are also too far away to attend school in the cities and towns. Instead, they can go to a *Telesecundaria*. Instead of being taught by a teacher, lessons are transmitted through a television in the classroom. In 1994, a powerful satellite was launched, which could reach even more remote villages. The new system had 6 channels, which were transmitted 24 hours a day.

Rising Numbers

In the late 1900s Mexico had one of the world's fastest-growing populations. Around 1910 the country had just fifteen million people. By 1990 that figure had grown to a huge 80 million. Around 2000 it passed the 100 million mark. In the last few years the birth rate has started to slow down.

This *maquiladora*, in the Mexican border town of Tijuana, produces cars and trucks that are mainly sold into the United States.

Time Off & Sports

Jai Alai

Jai alai is a fast-paced game. Players use curved rackets to strike the hard rubber ball. As in squash, the ball can be bounced off the walls of the court. The game comes from the Basque region of Spain.

What do Mexicans do in their free time, other than celebrating fiestas? You come across a game of soccer being played in a quiet alley.

Soccer crazy

Futbol (soccer) is Mexico's favorite sport. The game is played in every town and village and is wildly popular with fans. Top matches take place in venues such as the Azteca Stadium in Mexico City. The "Mexican wave" was invented here during the World Cup in 1986.

Jai alai is a fast-paced game – the *pelota* (ball) can travel up to 290 kph (190 mph)!

Other sports

Basketball, volleyball, and baseball are also very popular. Bullfighting has been part of Mexican culture for more than 500 years. Bullfights, called *corrida de toros* by Mexicans, generally begin on December 25, and they continue every Sunday until April.

Relaxing in Mexico

Some Mexicans keep fit by jogging. Whole families enjoy Spanish-style strolls, called *passeandos*, when temperatures cool in the evening. Towns such as Puebla have a lively nightlife, with bars, movie theaters, and nightclubs. Internet cafés are springing up even in small towns.

The Mayan Ball Game

The ancient Mayas had a ball game that was a cross between sport and a sacred ceremony. Two teams played with a rubber ball the size of a soccer ball. Players used hips and knees to bounce the ball though a hoop high on the wall. After the match, the losers, or sometimes the winners, were put to death in a religious **sacrifice**!

Mexican *futbol* fans enjoy the atmosphere at the 2002 World Cup in Japan.

The aim of the sacred Mayan ball game was to get the ball through a hoop like this one.

Travel & Cities

Rural transportation

You board a bus heading for Mexico City. The mix of vehicles on the road changes as you leave Puebla. Out in the countryside, donkeys, oxcarts, motorcycles, and bicycles are used to carry passengers and heavy loads.

Donkeys are used to help carry firewood in the countryside.

You are now eager to see more of Mexico. The capital, Mexico City, is your first destination. You stop in at the tourist office to find out about travel in Mexico.

On the road

The high mountain ranges make it difficult to build roads and railways that go across the country. Most major highways and rail routes run north to south, keeping to **plains** and valleys. The Pan-American highway runs the length of the country, linking Central America with the United States. Buses are one of the best ways of getting around, and also seeing the countryside. There are many different bus companies. Inside cities, people often use shared taxis to get around.

WORD BANK   plain large, flat area of land

Rail and air

Mexico's rail network dates back to the late 1800s. Rail travel is cheap but very unreliable. Only a few lines, such as the Copper Canyon railroad, run smoothly. Air travel is a great way of covering the huge distances inside Mexico for anyone who can afford the fares. Increasing numbers of people hop on a plane to travel between cities such as Mexico City, Monterrey, Merida, and Acapulco.

Colorful taxis are everywhere on this street in Mexico.

The Copper Canyon railroad runs for a total of 475 miles (700 kilometers).

The Copper Canyon Railroad

The rail route through the Copper Canyon has been called "the world's most scenic railroad." The 12-hour trip crosses 36 bridges and passes through 87 tunnels. On the way you see some of Mexico's most stunning scenery, including deep **gorges** and tumbling waterfalls.

gorge deep, narrow valley between hills or mountains

Sights of the Capital

Cathedral: the largest church in Mexico

National Palace: Site of Mexico's government

Templo Mayor: Remains of an Aztec temple

Latin American Tower: 44 stories high, the view from the top is fantastic

Palace of Fine Arts (below): holds some of Mexico's greatest art

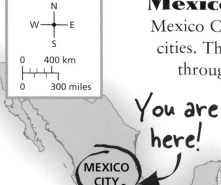

You are here!

MEXICO CITY

Mexico City

Mexico City is one of the world's largest cities. The bus takes a long time to weave through the **suburbs**. Eventually, you arrive in the center of Mexico's capital.

A historic city

Mexico City was founded by the Spanish in 1521. It is built on the ruins of the ancient Aztec capital, called Tenochtitlan, and on marshy land where a lake once stood. Mexico's capital has a mixture of Spanish **colonial**, 19th-century, and modern buildings. Buildings line the broad avenues that run through the city. As in other Mexican towns, the *zocalo* (main square) lies at the heart of the city.

pollution release of harmful chemicals into the air, ground, or water

Ups and downs

There's a lot to see in Mexico City, but the capital also has its problems. Heavy traffic makes it difficult to drive in the center. It's better to take the metro (subway) instead.

Pollution from cars and factories forms a blanket of smog (smoky fog) that hangs over the capital. Smog hides the surrounding mountains. On some days you can't even see the tops of tall buildings! To ease traffic jams and lower pollution levels, recent laws have made it more difficult for people to use their cars in the city.

That Sinking Feeling

Built on the soft, sandy bed of a drained lake, Mexico City is sinking. Just a century ago it stood 3 feet (1 meter) above the level of the lake. Now it is 10 feet (3 meters) below it. The city sinks about 6 inches (15 centimeters) every year.

The ground around Independence Monument in Mexico City is sinking rapidly.

Tequila

The town of Tequila, 31 miles (50 kilometers) west of Guadalajara, is where an alcoholic spirit of the same name was first made. Production of the drink started more than 200 years ago. It is made from blue agave, a cactus plant with long bluish-green spiky leaves. Fields of this plant surround the town.

Mexican cities

Besides the capital, Mexico has many other interesting cities that are worth a visit. You borrow a guide book to figure out where to head next.

A typical Mexican city

Guadalajara, to the west, is Mexico's second-largest city. Located in a high valley, it has a mild **climate**. The city has a small center with landmarks dating from the 1500s. Guadalajara is home to many typically Mexican things, including tequila and mariachi music, which can be heard all over town.

➤ The pace of life is relaxed in Guadalajara. Old Spanish buildings edge the squares.

Monterrey or Acapulco?

In the northeast, Monterrey is a busy city with spectacular rugged mountains surrounding it. There are huge squares with mainly modern architecture. A tall tower called the Beacon of Commerce shoots laser beams around the city at night.

In southwestern of Mexico, Acapulco is the country's most famous resort. It is known for its sandy beaches and lively nightlife. Although it is located on the Pacific coast, it is not that far from the capital. You decide to head for Acapulco. You pack your bags and hop on a bus.

▲ Divers plunge a massive 130 feet (40 meters) off the cliff at La Quebrada.

Divers of La Quebrada, Acapulco

Acapulco is famous for its daring divers, who plunge into the sea from a steep cliff called La Quebrada. Dives must be timed just right to catch the incoming waves, or the diver will land on the rocks underneath the surf!

Jose Clemente Orozco

Mexican artists such as Jose Clemente Orozco (1883–1949) were inspired by great events in history, such as the Mexican Revolution. Orozco's most famous painting, shown on p. 10, shows Miguel Hidalgo, who called for revolt against the Spanish. The artist's work can be seen in Guadalajara, and also in the United States, where he lived for a time.

N
W E
S
0   400 km
0   300 miles

You are here!

MEXICO CITY.

•Acapulco

City life

Even the lively, modern city of Acapulco has an old center, dating back to the early days of Spanish rule. Spanish ships used the port in the 1500s, bringing silk and spices from China and the Philippines.

Acapulco's old town lies behind the harbor. There's an old fort and a main square with a few public buildings. Some of these buildings are decorated with murals (wall paintings), often by famous artists such as Jose Clemente Orozco.

► This mural in the Presidential Palace is by Diego Rivera, one of Mexico's most famous artists.

HUELGA

shantytown area where the conditions are dirty and overcrowded, and houses are shacks

The number of people living in Mexican cities has grown rapidly in the last 50 years or so. In 1950 just 43 percent of Mexico's population lived in cities and towns. By 2000, more than 75 percent of all Mexicans were living in cities and towns.

This woman's home in the slums overlooks the glamour of Acapulco beach.

Expanding cities

Like many Mexican cities, Acapulco has grown a lot in recent years. Since the 1950s, huge numbers of Mexicans have moved to cities from **rural** areas, in search of work and a better life. However, many people end up without a job, living in the poor **shantytowns** (slums) that have grown up on the edges of cities. Homes in these slums, called "lost cities," have no electricity or running water. Even glitzy Acapulco has its share of slums.

rural to do with the countryside

Rural Life

You catch the bus back toward central Mexico. The road winds up the hills through farms and forests. Looking back, you can see fishing villages lining the blue coast.

Fishing

Fishing has been a major industry since the 1960s. The waters around Baja California are rich in tuna, sardines, anchovies, and red snapper. Shellfish such as squid and lobster are also caught. Shrimping, too, is big business along the Gulf of Mexico.

Harvesting Chicle

Tree sap called chicle, which is often still used to make chewing gum, comes from *sapodilla* trees grown on **plantations** in Mexico. The milky sap oozes from cuts in the bark. It is collected in little cups and then processed to make chewing gum.

A worker cuts into a *sapodilla* tree to harvest chicle.

WORD BANK   export when a country's products are sold abroad

Farming

You pass through rugged mountains where small farms dot the hillsides. Two main types of farming go on in Mexico. Most farms are small plots where local people grow corn, beans, squash, and potatoes to feed their families. At the other end of the scale are the big estates, where cotton, wheat, coffee, and sugarcane are grown for **export**.

Small-scale farmers work the land using hoes and other simple tools and plows pulled by horses. Large-scale farms can afford expensive machinery such as tractors and sprinkler systems to water the land.

Forestry

Many of Mexico's forests are being cut down for wood. The pine forests of central Mexico provide cheap timber. Valuable woods, such as pine and oak, grow in the rain forests of the southeast.

Ranching

Cattle are raised in parts of Mexico where the land is too poor to grow crops. In the north, farms raise beef cattle for their meat, some of which goes to the United States. Dairy cattle are raised on cleared forest land in the south.

These fishermen haul in their recent catch at a fishing harbor in Baja California.

plantation   area where crops such as tea, rubber, or *sapodilla* trees are grown

Market Day

You visit a local market, called a *tiangui*. People come from miles around to sell home-grown fruit and vegetables, handmade pottery and weaving. Also on show are cooking pots, cheap clothing, shoes, farm tools, and radios. You name it, you can buy it here!

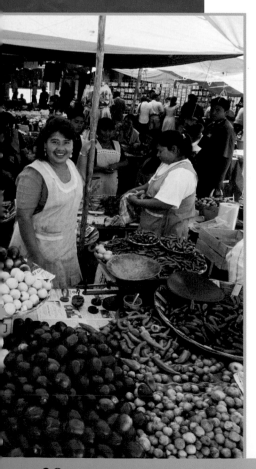

Country life

The beautiful scenery makes you decide to spend a few days in the countryside. The bus drops you in a tiny village. It's like entering another world!

Just about everything is different in the country. In cities, most Mexicans wear modern clothes. In the country, however, women wear long skirts, loose blouses, and *rebozos* (shawls). Men wear cotton shirts, pants, sandals, and sombreros. Most village houses are simple buildings one or two stories high. Some are made of adobe, which is a type of brick that is dried in the sun.

Village life

Most country people are farmers. Families keep a few animals such as chickens or a pig, mostly for their own needs. Any spare eggs, fruit, or vegetables are sold at the local market. Family life is important. Grandparents often live with their grown-up children and help raise the grandchildren. Young people often live at home until they get married.

Women in the countryside carry their babies in a sling made from a woven *rebozo*.

Land Rights

Since the revolution most farmland in Mexico has been owned **communally**. The shared land is called *ejidos*. Each farmer has rights over a small plot, which later passes to the farmer's children. Changes introduced in the 1990s mean that some farmers now own their land.

Mayan Ruins

The Yucatan has hundreds of Mayan sites, only some of which have been uncovered. Others still lie deep in the jungle! Palenque and Chichen Itza are the most visited. *La Ruta Maya* is a tourist trail linking the best sites.

At the local market you link up with a few other tourists. You go to a café to swap ideas about all the great places still left to visit in Mexico.

Spectacular ruins

At the top of the list for many tourists is a visit to one of Mexico's ancient cities. You can see Olmec ruins at La Venta in the south. The amazing city of Monte Alban in Oaxaca was built by the Zapotecs. The Mayas built temples all over the Yucatan. Experts are unsure who built the spectacular pyramids of Teotihuacan, 33 miles (50 kilometers) from Mexico City.

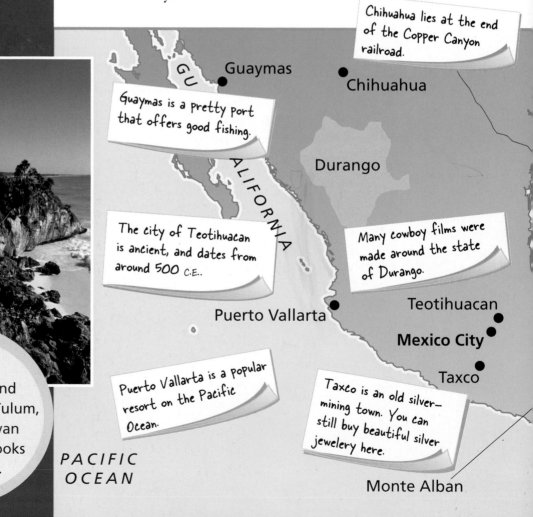

Combine swimming and sightseeing at Tulum, where a Mayan temple overlooks the beach.

Chihuahua lies at the end of the Copper Canyon railroad.

Guaymas is a pretty port that offers good fishing.

The city of Teotihuacan is ancient, and dates from around 500 C.E..

Many cowboy films were made around the state of Durango.

Puerto Vallarta is a popular resort on the Pacific Ocean.

Taxco is an old silver-mining town. You can still buy beautiful silver jewelery here.

Guaymas

Chihuahua

Durango

Puerto Vallarta

Teotihuacan

Mexico City

Taxco

Monte Alban

GU

ALIFORNIA

PACIFIC OCEAN

New horizons

Mexico is a huge country with very varied landscapes. You've seen parts of the Central **Plateau**, but the scenery elsewhere is also breathtaking. There are the cactus-dotted deserts of the north; the craggy mountains of the Sierra Madre; the lush rain forests of the southeast; and the blue, rocky *cenotes* of the Yucatan.

Flying Men of Papantla

At Papantla in east-central Mexico you can see the amazing dance of the *voladores*, or "flying men." Four men wearing bird costumes launch themselves from a high pole with ropes around their waists, and circle downward. It is seriously scary!

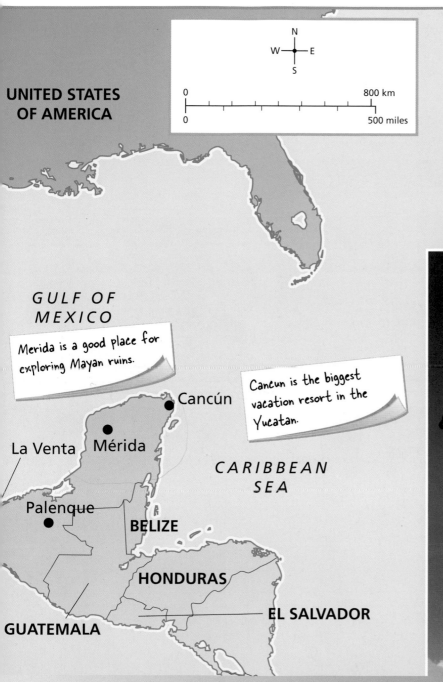

N
W • E
S

0   800 km

0   500 miles

UNITED STATES
OF AMERICA

GULF OF
MEXICO

Merida is a good place for exploring Mayan ruins.

Cancun is the biggest vacation resort in the Yucatan.

Cancún

La Venta   Mérida

CARIBBEAN
SEA

Palenque

BELIZE

HONDURAS

EL SALVADOR

GUATEMALA

Stay or Go Home?

You've seen a bit of Mexico, including Puebla, Acapulco, and the capital. But Mexico is a big place, and there is still a lot more to see and do! It's decision time—do you hop on a plane for home or sample more of Mexico?

Great days out

You make a list of must-do activities. It includes snorkeling at the coral reefs of the Yucatan, where you can also explore underground caves. On both the Pacific and Gulf coasts you can rent a boat to fish for tuna and marlin. Or you can paddle a kayak between islands off Baja California. You may even want to take a hike in the Copper Canyon or scale the great peak of Orizaba—the choice is yours!

Highlights of the National Parks (NP)

Agua Azul NP: jungle waterfalls

Sian Ka'an Reserve: tropical forests and mangrove swamps

Cascada de Basaseachic NP: Mexico's second-highest waterfall

Copper Canyon NP: fantastic canyon scenery

El Rosario, Michoacan: monarch butterfly sanctuary

Thousands of monarch butterflies cling to a tree in the Michoacan sanctuary.

WORD BANK lagoon pool of water by the sea

Wildlife watching

You haven't yet seen much of Mexico's wildlife. At El Rosario in Michoacan you can see monarch butterflies that have flown all the way from Canada. Scammon's **Lagoon** in Baja California is the place for whale watching. Gray whales give birth to their calves here in winter. You can catch a glimpse of monkeys and parrots in the rain forests. Flamingos and pelicans nest along the coast.

A gray whale and her calf enjoy the warm waters of Scammon's Lagoon.

Vacation Ideas

• Go white water rafting in Veracruz and visit the ruins of El Cuajilote, best seen from the river.

• Scuba dive off Cozumel Island in the Yucatan—one of the world's largest living coral reefs.

• Or you can dive to explore the underground caves of the Yucatan.

• Try rock climbing on sheer rock walls near Tijuana or Monterrey.

• Hike up the volcanic peak of *Iztaccihuatl* near Puebla.

mangrove swamp place in tropical regions where trees and shrubs grow in muddy areas near the sea

Find Out More

Eager Destination Detectives can find out more about Mexico by checking out the books and movies listed below.

Further reading

Garcia, James. *Cinco de Mayo*. Chanhassen, Minn.: Child's World, 2003.

Green, Jen. *Nations of the World: Mexico*. Chicago: Raintree, 2000.

McCulloch, Julie. *A World of Recipes: Mexico*. Chicago: Heinemann Library, 2001.

Park, Ted. *Taking Your Camera to Mexico*. Chicago: Raintree, 2000.

Parker, Edward. *The Changing Face of Mexico*. Chicago: Raintree, 2002

Films

Like Water for Chocolate (1992)
An epic story of love and loyalty during revolutionary times in northern Mexico.

Night of the Iguana (1964)
A haunting adventure set in Mexico. This American director's long fascination with Mexico began with the classic film *Treasure of the Sierra Madre* (1948).

World Wide Web

If you want to find out more about Mexico, you can search the Internet using keywords such as these:

• Mexico
• Yucatan Peninsula
• Mexico City

You can also find your own keywords by using headings or words from this book. Try using a search directory such as **yahooligans.com**.

Time Line

around 300–900 C.E.
Mayan culture flourishes in southeastern Mexico

1340s
Aztecs found the city of Tenochtitlan (now Mexico City) and rule a large empire from this capital

1519
An army of Spanish *conquistadors* (soldiers) led by Hernan Cortes lands on the Gulf coast and heads toward the Aztec capital

1521
Spanish *conquistadors* conquer Tenochtitlan. The Aztec empire becomes the core of the Spanish colony of New Spain. Spain rules Mexico for nearly 300 years.

1540s
The Spanish discover gold in New Spain. Huge amounts of gold and silver are shipped over to Spain.

1810
Miguel Hidalgo y Costilla begins Mexico's struggle for independence with his speech, the *grito de Dolores* ("cry from Dolores").

1867–1872
Maximilian is overthrown and Benito Juarez becomes president again

1862
France invades Mexico. Mexican troops defeat France at the Battle of Puebla, but the French win later the same year. They make an Austrian archduke, Maximilian, emperor. He rules for three years.

1855–64
A lawyer called Benito Juarez, from the Zapotec Indian tribe, is president of Mexico

1846–1848
The United States wins a war against Mexico and takes much of Mexico's territory

1836
The Mexican territory of Texas wins independence and becomes part of the United States

1821
Mexico wins independence after eleven years of fighting

1876–1911
The dictator Porfirio Diaz now rules Mexico

1910–1917
The Mexican Revolution takes place. The revolutionaries overthrow Porfirio Diaz.

1917
Mexico adopts its constitution

1929
The National Revolutionary Party (PRM) is formed and wins control of Mexico. In 1946 it becomes the Institutional Revolutionary Party (PRI). It remains in power until the year 2000.

1934–1940
President Lazaro Cardenas of the PRM introduces many new changes, including giving back land once owned by farmers

1958
Mexican women get the vote for the first time

2000
The PRI loses the elections. President Vicente Fox of the National Action Party is elected. Mexico makes a new free trade agreement with the European Union.

1994
Indian revolutionaries from the state of Chiapas revolt, demanding better living conditions

1993
Mexico and the United States make an important trade agreement, called the North American Free Trade Agreement (NAFTA)

1988
Hurricane Gilbert strikes the Yucatan Peninsula, killing about 200 people

1985
A major earthquake hits Mexico City, killing 6,000 people

1968
Mexico hosts the Olympic Games

45

Mexico: Facts & Figures

Mexico's flag has been used since 1821, when Mexico became independent from Spain. It has three vertical stripes: green for independence, white for religion, and red for union (left to right). The coat of arms in the center represents a legend; the Aztecs built their capital, Tenochtitlan (now Mexico City), where they saw an eagle sitting on a cactus eating a snake.

People and Places

- Population: 104.9 million.
- Mexico City is the oldest capital city in the Americas and the largest capital city in the world.
- Average life expectancy: 74.9 years

Money Matters

- Average earnings:
  Men: US$13,152
  (£7,473)
  Women: US$4,978
  (£2,828)

What's in a Name?

- Mexico's original name was Meshtleeko. However, the Spanish conquistadors could not pronounce this, and so changed the name to Mexico! The official name of Mexico is Estados Unidos Mexicanos or the United Mexican States.

Food and Health

- Mexico introduced chocolate to the world.
- The Spanish brought the smallpox illness to Mexico, which killed many of the Indians.
- The average Mexican drinks more bottles of Coca Cola in a day than any other nationality in the world!

Glossary

active volcano that may erupt sometime in the future

barren bare land, with very little growing on it

Catholocism the Roman Catholic religion, a form of Christianity

cavalry soldiers on horses

climate regular pattern of weather in a region

colony country that is controlled by another ruling country

communally owned by all the people who work on it

compulsory something you have to do

dictator ruler who governs without having been elected by the people

dormant volcano that is not expected to erupt again

empire group of countries ruled by a single country or ruler

export when a country's products are sold abroad

fertile land that is good for growing crops on

gorge deep, narrow valley between hills or mountains

hurricane fierce storm with very high winds

independence freedom from control by another country

inhabitant someone who lives in a place

lagoon pool of water by the sea

mangrove swamp place in tropical regions where trees and shrubs grow in muddy areas near the sea

mineral substance found in the ground, such as gold, silver, and zinc

patron saint saint who is believed to protect a place, job, or activity

peninsula area of land that is mostly surrounded by water

plain large, flat area of land

plantation area where crops such as tea, rubber, or *sapodilla* trees are grown

plateau area of high, flat land

pollution release of harmful chemicals into the air, ground, or water

porous rock that has tiny holes so that water can trickle through it

relief map map that shows where the land is higher or lower

rural to do with the countryside

sacrifice something that is killed and offered to a god

scrubland area covered in small trees and bushes

shantytown area where the conditions are dirty and overcrowded, and houses are shacks

suburb built-up area on the edge of a town or city

tectonic plate one of the huge slabs of rock that make up Earth's outer layer, which is called the crust

territory land that a country or ruler owns or controls

trench deep furrow or ditch in the ground

Index